The MYSTICAL POEMS of KABIR

The
MYSTICAL
POEMS
of
KABIR

Translation and Commentary by
Swami Rama
and Robert B. Regli

The Himalayan International Institute
of Yoga Science and Philosophy
of the U.S.A.
Honesdale, Pennsylvania

Himalayan International Institute
of Yoga Science and Philosophy of the U.S.A.
RR 1, Box 400
Honesdale, Pennsylvania 18431

First Printing 1990

Cover photo by Dave Gorman

Kabir, 15th cent.
     [Poems. English. Selections]
     The mystical poems of Kabir / Swami Rama and Robert Regli.
        p. cm.
     ISBN 0-89389-121-5 : $8.95
     I. Rama, Swami, 1925–   . II. Regli, Robert, 1958–
III. Title.
PK2095.K3A233 1990
891'.4312—dc20
                                           90-20832
                                              CIP

Contents

Acknowledgments

We thank Pandit Usharbudh Arya, D.Litt., for generously helping us obtain Hindi versions of Kabir's poetry. We also thank Devika Nichols for manuscript preparation and word processing, Darlene Clark for typesetting, Vicki Roser for layout and design, and Gopala Deva for printing.

About Kabir and His Poetry

Very little is known about Kabir and his life, but we can still enjoy his poems just as they are enjoyed by many, all over the world. Kabir is as much a favorite today as he was five hundred years ago, and the lessons he shares in his poetry are just as applicable now as in the fifteenth century when they were written. Actually, after reading them, one might think that Kabir was directly addressing our present spiritual and religious crisis.

It is unfortunate that Kabir is so little-known in the Western hemisphere, because Westerners would be delighted by his philosophical and mystical poetry. Kabir was a great Indian sage, seer, and poet. Those who are poets enjoy Kabir's verse, while those who are musicians sing and play his music. His many poems are set in *ragas* (classical music) that can be enjoyed by all lovers of music. Westerners would benefit from the study of Kabir's life, poetry, and sayings, for they are unique in the literature of the world. But to truly understand Kabir, you would need a Kabir to explain a Kabir, and where is such a great soul today?

Sometimes Kabir speaks of the highly evolved yogic and mystical experiences received by the adepts; sometimes he speaks of the path of love, which can be trod by men of common intelligence. Sometimes he condemns fanatics and hypocrites—he doesn't spare anyone in the pursuit of

1

the pure, clear philosophy and wisdom of the Divine.

To simply translate Kabir's verses into English would make little new contribution to literature, since many other English translations already exist, although none are in rhyming verse. With the goal in mind of helping modern people easily remember Kabir's verses, we endeavored to rhyme them. We were careful not to distort the originality of Kabir's poems, or to alter his thoughts or philosophy in any manner. In rhyming these verses, we chose a direct and personal language, so that readers may be uplifted and inspired by his poetry. We also carefully used simple English words, so that the verses do not become too intricate or complicated, since the poems and sayings are already often highly mystical. The original verses were written in Hindi, in the devanagari script used in the fifteenth century.

There was a time when I taught Kabir's poetry and philosophy from the viewpoint of *sadhana,* and his views on sadhana became a part of my own practical philosophy and are dear to me. Therefore, in this volume, we decided to select and organize his poems systematically, on the basis of subject matter, such as yogic sadhana, *nirguna bhakti,* and other related topics, rather than in chrono-logical order.

In this undertaking, we have carefully examined all the literature available in Hindi, English, and Urdu and se-lected poems considered to be authentic by scholars who have studied Kabir's literature in those languages. We tried to determine the original meaning and content of poems attributed to Kabir, because in India writers have tended to alter the sayings of the sages, and when translated, some distortions of nuance often creep in. These distortions are called *ksepaks* (additions), and they can be found in

Tulsidas' *Ramayana* as well as in the writings attributed to Meera and in other literature of the bhakti movement. Most of this material has been drawn from two references sources: *Kabir Granthavali* and the *Gyan Bijak*. These two books seem to be the most authentic, although we examined sakis and songs, and finally chose as our primary sources the two above-mentioned books.

Drawing on all the available resources, we will attempt to provide a summary of what little is known about Kabir's life and circumstances. Yet ultimately, we are dependent on Kabir's poetry itself for what we know of him and his teachings.

Historians and writers have differed in their statements regarding Kabir's heritage, but in his verse, he himself claims to have been a Kori, a low-caste Hindu, who was born into a weaver's family:

Harai konam abhe pad datta
Kahe kori Kabira;
Mera ramke abhe pad nagari
Kahe Kabira Juhla ha.

And in another location, he himself says, *"Purav janm hum brahman hote/Oche karm tap hena,"* indicating that in a previous birth he had been a Brahmin, but had not done the requisite austerities, nor had his actions been appropriate as a Brahmin. He goes on to say that he had not properly served his master—that is, his spiritual preceptor—and so he was subsequently reborn into a low-caste family of weavers.

Many scholars—including Shyam Sundar Das, Ram Kuma Varma, and Hazari Prasad Dvivedi—believe Kabir was born into a Hindu family and brought up by a Muslim family. A few scholars have written that Kabir was born of a Brahmin widow, but could furnish no evidence to support this. Some scholars say Kabir's father was Muslim, deeply influenced by yogis. Other scholars say his father's name was not Niru, as was generally believed, but rather Gosain.

There is much controversy over Kabir's birthdate, but one poem that is attributed to Kabir's disciple Dharamdas states that Kabir was born on a Monday during the full moon in July, in Vikram Samvit 1455, which is equivalent to A.D. 1398. Kabir's guru, Swami Ramananda, dropped his body in V.S. 1470, which would have made Kabir approximately fifteen years of age at the time. Kabir was said to have been initiated by his master when he was twelve years old.

There is a similar disagreement about Kabir's birthplace: some scholars believe he was born at Varanasi; others believe at Magahar. Still another group of scholars believe he was born at Ajamgarh, in the village of Belhara. But Kabir himself says: *"Pahile darshan kashi payo, Puni magahar vase ie,"* indicating that he met his revered preceptor (Swami Ramananda) first at Varanasi, and then later moved to Magahar. Kabir's disciple Dharamdas also says that Kabir was from Varanasi, which was at that time called Kashi.

Varanasi has long been a seat of learning, especially of spiritual learning, and even today it is seen as a center of education. During that time there was much social upheaval and political turmoil created by alien invaders. The people of India experienced serious conflict created by both the rigidity of Brahmanism and the fundamentalism of Islam. Kabir fearlessly advocated and propagated his philosophy, which rejected the worst of both.

Muslims say that Kabir was a disciple of Sheikh Taqqi, while Hindus claim that he was a disciple of Swami Ramananda. It is clear that Kabir was a disciple of Ramananda, for Sheikh Taqqi's name is mentioned only once by Kabir, while Ramananda's name is frequently mentioned with great respect and reverence. In his poetry Kabir said that reverence for the guru comes first, even before reverence for God; therefore, had he been a disciple of Sheikh Taqqi, references to the Sheikh would probably have appeared more prominently in his poems.

Kabir was married to a woman named Loi-Dhanya. Some scholars, however, believe that he had two wives: Loi as the first, Dhanya as the second. Kabir had a son and a daughter, whose names he states as Kamaal and Kamaali, respectively.

Like Buddha, Guru Nanak Dev, and Charu Vak, Kabir was actually one of the great reformers of his time. Throughout history, the call of time and necessity has given birth to great souls. Kabir was such a sage, born when Brahmins, the teaching class, were involved in rigidity and rituals, forgetting real spirituality and true philosophy. Great thinkers, including the Buddha, Swami Dayananda, and Raja Ram Mohan Rai, among others, had openly criticized and condemned the contemporary rituals and priesthood of India, asserting that the priesthood was damaging the noble spiritual heritage of India and its culture. Other sages in the South, in Bengal, and in Maharashtra had also expounded Vedic philosophy and culture in Marati, Tamil, Malayan, and Bengali.

Two streams of thought have flowed simultaneously from the Vedic period up to the modern day. One approach values the combination of knowledge *(jnana)* and devotion *(bhakti);* the other approach emphasizes the performance of rituals *(karma kanda)*. Kabir's philosophy mingled jnana and bhakti, but he bitterly opposed the ritualistic cult practiced by the Brahmins.

To fully understand Kabir's era, we must recall that during this time, there was fierce rivalry between Hindus and Muslims. Kabir tried to create a bridge between these two diverse cultures. The Islamic forces had moved into India around the seventh century A.D., and by Kabir's time (the fifteenth century A.D.), Islamic leaders had begun to use violence to force the Hindu masses to Muslim ways. Due to this violence, the Hindus chose to adopt the veil system *(purdah,* or *parda)* as a way of providing safety for the women. Among Hindus, women were considered to be the goddesses of the family and the custodians of their culture and civilization. Hindu culture and society, in spite of attacks from aliens and invaders, have long remained essentially intact because of the role played by women, who were not influenced by alien cultures. The Muslims (and later the British) tried their best to influence Hindu culture and to convert the masses using violent tactics. Although they were successful in converting some Hindus, they could never achieve complete success because the Indian women remained unyielding in their steadfast adherence to Hindu culture and religion.

By the fifteenth century, Hindu society had inevitably disintegrated to a certain extent during the period of alien rule. Unfortunately, it thus became easy for the alien Muslim (and later, the British) invaders to strike at the culture's weak point and convert the downtrodden, mostly the lowest-class Shudras. Works by artists such as Tulsi and Sur, the great poets and seers of India, were suppressed, so that their poems and songs, which were composed in the simple Hindi vernacular, could not inspire the masses to agitate for the freedom of India. Nonetheless, these works remained highly revered and have survived intact to this day. Schoolchildren in India still recite Kabir's poems, which are easily memorized and have always been extremely popular.

During Kabir's time only Brahmins and a few scholars knew Sanskrit, the language in which all the religious and spiritual scriptures were written; the masses spoke Hindi. Kabir himself did not have a formal education, but acquired much experience and knowledge by meditating and conversing with *sadhus* from many different orders, including that of Shankara. Because of this influence, some of Kabir's poetry also condensed the Vedantic philosophy for the masses.

KABIR'S PHILOSOPHY

Contemporary intellectuals and scholars greatly respect Kabir not only for the poetic heights he reached, but also for his mystical and intellectual depth. The philosophy presented in his works is identical to that of the Upanishads—there exists a nameless, formless, absolute Reality, One without a second. A reader who is well-versed in the Upanishadic literature may be able to tell from the poems that Kabir understood the depths of the Upanishadic philosophy because of *satsanga*[1] with the sadhus and the assembly of spiritual people.

The world's largest collection of religious literature belongs to the Hindu society. This literature includes the *Vedas, Puranas, Upanishads, Bhagavad Gita,* and tantric and yogic literature. It is said that if someone decided to

[1]To converse with and be in the presence of *sadhus* (saints and sages).

thoroughly study all of this literature, it would take at least 10,000 years, and that the scholar would have to be born again and again to actually read it all.

One outstanding fact of Hinduism is that its adherents do not criticize or discount the other religions that are practiced or followed by non-Hindus. Hindus are traditionally very liberal in their religious concepts. To quote the *Upanishads:* "*Basudhaivan kutumbakam*—The whole world is our family and all creatures are members of our family."

Thus, an important attribute of Hinduism is that every Hindu is free to think and believe the way he or she wants. A more subtle point is that all are free in their personal religious concepts and thinking process, even though in their external personal life they may not be completely free to marry whomever they want. Hindus desire to create families that are strong units and yet provide individuals with freedom in their ways of religious belief, philosophical thinking, and method of worship. For instance, in one family a father may worship Lord Shiva, while the mother worships Durga, the son worships Krishna, and the daughter-in-law worships Rama. Yet still, all the members of the family follow the traditional culture, which is perhaps the most ancient on earth.

Such freedom may be beneficial for individual scholars and thinkers, but it also created a serious conflict and lack of integration in Hindu society, like a split or a division in a many-storied mansion. Kabir was concerned about the multiplicity of Hindu shrines and temples; the diversity of shrines and variety of religious approaches did not provide a sense of social cohesiveness, so the Indian people were not unified in their spiritual beliefs.

India today still suffers on account of this inherent

problem and politicians often exploit this situation. Today India needs Kabir's and Guru Nanak Dev's philosophy, which can be understood by the common masses. This philosophy will certainly create a bridge between the divisive "isms" that have plagued India for many centuries.

India's political, religious, and social leaders do not have the understanding and commitment to bring the different provinces together into a unified stream. It is amazing to note that people still do not want to say that they are "Indian" but will instead say that they are Bengalis, Punjabis, Madrasis, or Kashmiris. This clearly shows that the states see themselves as separate, with languages and cultures that are different in many ways. Although their shrines and places of worship have the same philosophical background, they look different and their modes of worship differ as well.

Instead of resolving these major problems, Indian leaders have allowed their society to suffer due to a lack of vision. The sayings of Kabir and Guru Nanak Dev, translated into many different languages and circulated to the different states of India, will help people to understand the real philosophies of India—unity in diversity; and equality, not disparity. Yet, it is difficult to achieve this task, because even after forty-three years of freedom, the leaders of India have not solved certain inherent ills and guided the nation in a unifying manner. Although India is a melting pot, the multiplicity of shrines, the different languages and tongues, and the diverse cultures have prevented anything solid from emerging from the melting pot that could help to unite the nation.

Kabir's writings will be as valuable to modern Indians as they were five hundred years ago. Westerners and

Western scholars do not know much about Indian philosophy, because the descriptions of Indian philosophy and religion produced by Western missionaries often reflect their own biased opinions.

Since the time of the creation of Pakistan, Indian and Pakistani historians have still not been able to settle their historical differences. No matter what country we visit and which culture we study, we see that cultural heritage plays a great role in human life—customs, systems, and traditions all meet and weave the fabric of a culture. Education is the only means of creating communication. Yet in India today, texts that openly condemn women and their status are still being taught in the schools, and the same old history that was written by British historians is still taught in colleges, even after forty-three years of independence.

In his own time, Kabir was a poet, sage, and reformer, who openly condemned disparity on all dimensions, and was among those who were free from dogma and fanaticism. The *Bhagavad Gita* says that whenever there is degeneration and decay in society, a leader appears. That is certainly true in the case of Kabir. Like Guru Nanak Dev, who was another great sage, Kabir propagated the ideals of unity. Hail to these sages!

Wherever he went, Kabir held *satsanga* sessions. He became quite famous for his poetic sayings, which were easily memorized and recited. Classical musicians idolized Kabir for his songs, which are profound, beautiful, and inspiring, with deep spiritual and yogic meaning. He is considered to be one of the greatest of all mystic poets. We cannot really compare Kabir with any other sage of India—he is unique and without peer. Guru Nanak Dev, the founder of the Sikh tradition, so greatly admired Kabir's poetry that the *Adi Granth*, the Sikhs' main scriptural text, frequently quotes Kabir's verses. Although Kabir's guru, Swami Ramananda, was a renowned Vaishnava, Kabir simplified Vedanta philosophy with the path of *nirguna bhakti*, just as Madh Sudan Saraswati introduced a blend of bhakti and Vedanta. Thus, as a poet/philosopher, he took the role of the "lost lover" of the *nirguna bhakti* school, which emphasizes devotion to the Absolute One. In his verse, Kabir takes the Lord as his beloved and also addresses the Lord as his husband. Devotional verse, such as that composed by the Sufis at this time, commonly employed the analogy of the lover/beloved or wife/husband to express the yearning of the seeker for his Lord. This analogy also reflects the relationship of *jiva*, the individual soul, with her consort Brahman, the Absolute Reality. In addition, Kabir refers to the Lord as his mother, father, guru, and master in the same way that Tulsi Das does.

Kabir was also a great meditator, who had direct yogic experience of his own internal states, and was a sage with multidimensional abilities. In his teaching, Kabir emphasized the path of meditation without an object. Through his verses, Kabir ridicules hypocrites or "fakers" but always respects true *fakirs*. As he says, "You might spend your time telling beads, but you will not attain anything, because your heart and mind remain impure."

Kabir's spiritual sadhana was actually purely yogic, and involved an understanding of the *chakras*, as explained in ancient yogic manuals. He uses such terms as *asthakamal* (eight-petaled lotus), *charka dole* (the wheel), and also mentions *ida, pingala,* and *sushumna,* (the nadis) which, according to the yogic system, are the three major energy channels in the human body. He also speaks of nectar flowing from the crown of the head. These are all yogic terms and principles, which he used to explain his own internal states. Thus, Kabir was a great example for the yogis, renunciates, and householders equally.

In his ability to draw value from many diverse sources, Kabir was actually like a bee who tapped the nectar from many different flowers and converted it into honey. His philosophy developed and spread at a time when yogic sadhana was practiced mostly by the *Nath Panthis* and other yogic sects. His philosophy was influenced by the Nath Panthi yogis, who practiced a type of kundalini and tantra yoga. It is difficult to judge whether Kabir was influenced much by Sufism, which was just beginning to gain popularity during his time, although Sufism itself borrowed many of its spiritual ethics from the Upanishads.

When Kabir discussed sadhana he emphasized yogic sadhana; he didn't believe in the externalization of spirituality in the form of rituals or worship, but emphasized internal devotion and meditation. Prior to this time, the common masses of India did not understand the deeper aspects of yogic sadhana, and Kabir's verses helped to popularize the yogic philosophy of life and the art of living and being.

Kabir's sadhana was *bhakti sadhana* but his version of bhakti differs from that of other poets because of his unique expression of nirguna bhakti. Nirguna bhakti emphasizes love without an object or specific personification and meditation without an object, rather than bhakti and devotion only for a personified form of the Divine. For Kabir, nirguna bhakti is the means of final liberation. On this path, the *satguru* (a true master) and satsanga are the only real means for liberation. Kabir's philosophy went beyond caste, creed, sex, and color. After he left his body in A.D. 1518, his followers formed a *Kabir Panth* (The

Path of Kabir) to continue the teachings of his tradition. The Kabir Panth still exists today but is not very active.

It has been said that every poet has a touch of mysticism, but Kabir's poetry is both highly mystic and at the same time, realistic. Although scholars and musicians have repeatedly praised the poetry of Kabir to the fullest extent of their capacity, still no one has successfully painted a true and entire picture of Kabir. Acharya Ram Chandra has said that there are two distinct paths of spirituality: one is the path of knowledge and the other is the path of ecstasy. Kabir's philosophy and poetry inseparably weave together these threads of knowledge and ecstasy. For Kabir, the goal is *sahaja samadhi*, a state of mind attained through spontaneous ecstasy.

We hope that readers all over the world will be uplifted and inspired by Kabir's poetry. We would be happy to receive from the reader any suggestions for additions or improvements for the next edition of this book.

Peeking Within

The musk deer searches through the forest trees
For the fragrance that will enchant and please;

But all the while it searches, never knowing,
From its own nature the musk is flowing.

So, too, the Lord is within every being,
But outside we seek Him and live without seeing.

§

The Limitless is not limited to any space;
His presence pervades in every place.

For those who know the Lord is near at hand,
Close to those He will always stand.

For those who insist, far away the Lord must be,
No doubt very distant from those is He.

§

The Lord is far away, my old thoughts had begun,
But now I know the Lord abides in everyone.

For those who do know not who they truly are,
Though the Lord is close by, for them He is quite far.

§

Leaving their fields, where they've been plowing,
Men gather at temples for ritual bowing.

But the Lord does dwell within your heart;
Enter His temple and never depart.

§

Searching

If sincerely you seek to learn the Lord's name
Your ego will be consumed by its flame.

Come into the fire if you are ready to burn;
Your whole life is at stake, it is this you must learn.

§

Searching through the world I did once begin,
Looking for the sinners and places that they sin.

I searched upon the seas and all across the ground
But all that I had searched for, never could be found.

Then once I searched within I could clearly see—
Every sin or evil lies within me.

§

Gathered rocks that once had been strewn,
They are chiseled, shaped, and precisely hewn.

Stones for these temples are carefully laid;
Inside idols stand, each out of stone made.

But rock will crumble and fall apart,
Making rock idols useless from the start.

How can they help anyone to cross
This stormy sea, with waves of chaos?

§

Like grains of sand and sugar, hard to separate
The deluded mind has no power to discriminate.

The elephant's tusk can't separate the two;
Yet the humble ant knows clearly what to do.

Kabir says: Pride cannot be washed out of the mind;
Lovingly seek truth, and the Lord you will find.

§

I searched behind many blades of grass;
I searched the highest peak, beyond the mountain pass.

Looking for the Lord, I searched high and low;
I never found Him out there, now I know.

Once in the company of the master, truth finally came:
He revealed the Light within me; now I'll never be the
    same.

§

Far and wide did I search for the Lord;
Mountains I climbed, rivers did I ford.

But when the presence of the Lord was found,
My perspective of the world changed around.

§

In search for God, the experts look
In scriptures, texts, and holy books,

But pride alone grows with scholarly deeds;
And to their downfall does this lead.

§

As long as my thoughts always dwelt on me,
The Lord I was never able to see.

I no longer exist, only You are;
I no longer exist, only You are.

§

Journeying off to a holy place,
Fasting, while seeking the Lord's grace,

Bathing in frigid waters that take your breath—
Men have done austerities 'till their death.

But all this becomes a foolish game
Unless one knows the true divine name.

As food for death are all such men;
They come and depart, again and again.

§

What good do baptisms and holy baths do;
Can water make the mind serene and true?

From such water the fish never leave;
Bathing does not their odor relieve.

§

Those giving to charity, expecting a return,
Will be born as elephants on the next turn,

In the stables of the wealthy and the elite
Where a hoard of food is available to eat.

§

For lost lovers of God I've searched around,
But true lovers of the Lord are rarely found.

When true lovers together come,
Poison will eternal nectar become.

§

The Word

Within yourself, music plays without pause;
Vibrating strings are not the cause.

This music comes from the Word, says Kabir;
It pervades subtly for all to hear.

This sound divine makes the seeker free,
Then in maya's clasp he shall no more be.

§

The Word is more than a simple word so plain;
Through power of the Word no bondage will remain.

The Word is soothing, melting all desires;
It douses the flames of earthly fires.

But all other words provide only pain;
No peace or truth can they help you attain.

§

The value of the Word no treasure comes near;
Only the true disciple knows this truth, says Kabir.

Rubies and sapphires can easily be sought,
But the name of the Lord cannot be bought.

§

For this suffering world you find me crying,
For the pathetic world you find me sighing.

But the one who knows the Word will be
The only one who will cry with me.

§

The Word is so powerful it can inspire,
Even the kings to renounce and retire.

§

One who has stopped and sought carefully to see
The meaning of the Word, very fortunate is he.

Pitch darkness persists without the Word;
Where can you go if you haven't heard?

§

Until one finds the Word's door,
He's aimlessly wandering forevermore.

Over the world, doubt has control;
One having mastered it is a rare soul.

There is a way out of doubt's wrath:
Learning the Word is the only path.

§

The master has built a beautiful mansion,
Especially designed for spiritual expansion.

For a glimpse of the Beloved in this castle so high,
A ray of his Light the Lord did supply.

§

The dark mysteries of night go away
When the sun rises to start the day—

Just as when Light enters your heart,
Then, doubt and delusion all depart.

§

Philosophy

The waves swell and fall, again and again,
Just as death and then birth absorb all men.

Praiseworthy is he, free from karma's wheel,
To whom the Lord, the truth will reveal.

§

Laws of Providence are natural and pure:
For all who are born, departure is sure.

Fools see this life as its only end;
The wise use this life as a means, my friend.

§

I am sad to see that over all the land
The evil and wicked are in total command.

Listen, Kabir, and now take heart:
They will receive their exact part,

For all the seeds that they do drop
Will return to them in a future crop.

§

Celebrate life while you have it, Kabir;
Use wisely the time in which you are here.

When a ripe fruit falls to the ground
Back on the branch it will never be found.

§

For the right time, O Kabir, just wait;
All things happen at their own rate.

Flooding the field, the farmer may find,
At the wrong season, is ill-timed.

§

The human heart suffers separation from the Lord;
The goal of unity is what you journey toward.

This experience is a must for one to see
Fulfillment of purpose and the desire to be free.

§

Death brings a fear to mankind,
But brings great joy to my mind.

Kabir says: Only when we finally cease
Do we achieve perfect joy and peace.

§

To the one whose thorn has pierced you,
Bring a blossom, fresh with dawn dew.

For you, the flower will soon return
While a larger thorn will your enemy earn.

§

You are born to grow and learn;
With sincere efforts you should earn.

Think wisely about what you do;
This moment will not come back to you.

§

What happens next, we do not know,
Yet future seeds we always sow.

Death is swift when it comes your way,
Like a hawk that pounces on its prey.

§

Be friendly and warm to others you meet,
With full reverence, you should them greet.

Say aloud, "Yes, yes," to what they say,
But within yourself you should not sway.

§

From one color do all colors come;
And yet all color proceeds from One.

From what color is life begun?
Contemplate well on this.

§

The body which doesn't give love regard,
Is dead, you see, like a graveyard.

Though the blacksmith's bellows blow in and out,
Still any life they are without.

One by one, each of your loved ones go;
Soon, my friend, will come your final blow.

§

What to make of this world of ours?
First it's sweet; later it sours.

Yesterday a grand palace they possessed,
But now in the graveyard they helplessly rest.

§

Only the Lord of Life, says Kabir,
Should one love and always hold dear.

To this world, disgusting and untrue,
Remain unattached, all the way through.

How can one tell what years the goat lived for?
It still waits its turn at the butcher's door.

§

Analogy

If you a sleeping sadhu find,
Wake him to a meditative mind.

But there are three others one should not wake:
These are a fool, a tiger, and a snake.

§

The wave, the river, and the ocean are the same—
Only one source exists from which all came.

As the wave's height swells,
Still as water it dwells.

When the ocean's wave subsides
As water it still resides.

Wave is just a name;
It's water still the same.

§

Water freezes into snow;
Back to water it will go.

It is now what it was before;
Say nothing else, there is nothing more.

§

Why do things and forget
So that later you regret?

When you plant the bitter babul seed in the ground
Don't expect sweet mangoes on the tree to be found.

§

A flawless diamond is offered for gold;
Not knowing its value, it remains unsold.

The flawless diamond lay on the ground;
Enveloped with dust, it couldn't be found.

But the wise one who knows the value of this stone
Will take this priceless gem as his own.

§

Brilliant pearls and gems are strewn along the way;
The ignorant may see them, but still they go away.

For them the Light of lights doesn't shine anywhere;
They delight in darkness and remain unaware.

§

Kabir says: Remain separate from the world,
Like oil from water when together swirled.

Place your heart, Kabir insists,
Where neither death nor time exists.

§

Remembering the
Lord's Name

In any situation with problems or pain
The devoted student remembers the Lord's name.

Only the sage remembers the Lord at a joyous time;
If everyone did the same, no grief would they find.

For such a disciple, one could say,
That pain and pleasure do not affect his way.

§

Women balance water jars to and from the well.
They glide along so gracefully, and a story they tell.

Toward home they joke and laugh all the way;
Not a drop is lost, their attention doesn't stray.

Likewise the Lord's name one should remember true,
Not forgetting a moment, day and night through.

§

Watch the grazing cow wander in the grass so tall:
Her mind is on her calf, back inside the stall.

Kabir says: Perform your actions lovingly, and do the
    same;
In every breath of life, remember His name.

§

Gold and jewels are always on the thief's mind;
His mind is on them constantly, every moment he can find.

Keep the Lord's name in your mind the same way,
While fulfilling your duties during the day.

§

Frantically flapping its wings with all its might,
The moth kills itself in the bright candlelight.

With such concentration remember His name,
Amid thick and thin, pleasure and pain.

§

Devotion

Regardless of man's worldly position
The seed of devotion will come to fruition.

A gold pendant holds value wherever it's hung,
Even if dropped in a pile of dung.

§

It's a useless and a hopeless notion,
To think liberation does not need devotion.

Of the millions of methods one can try,
All are a waste, as time will pass by.

Only he who has merged into His name
Will dwell in His home and know of His fame.

§

Many do mortifications and boast of the path they've
    known;
As a crowd you can see them, bowing down to a stone.

Kabir says: By devotion alone the Lord has come to me;
Through purifying my heart, meeting the Lord came to be.

§

The path of love, all should hear,
Is for those rare ones, all sincere.

The path doesn't favor the slow or the fast;
It cares not for status, religion, or caste.

Who remembers His name without a pause—
Rare is he who obeys Divine laws.

§

The path of true devotion is delicate and divine,
Like walking on a razor's edge, a dangerous thin line.

If honesty and reverence are not very strong
Then the student on the path does not persist for long.

§

No sense of superiority exists in devotion;
All pride and all ego cease in this emotion.

Devotion consists of true reverence and love;
Respect adds its voice, with strength from above.

Devotion with love that's firm, true, and strong,
Is as rare as a rainbow, as melodious as a song.

§

Climbing love's ladder leads to liberation;
Fearlessly the sages climb, with no hesitation.

Lazy, selfish people love's ladder can't ascend;
The limits of their ego they never shall transcend.

§

Kabir says: Many foolish methods are patently absurd;
Only he attains the goal who practices the Word.

When meditative practice is steady and sincere,
Only then will mindfulness and harmony appear.

§

Health, wealth, and pleasure, you can desire—
Fleeting at best, though many aspire.

But deep meditation and contentment with duty
Are treasures far greater than all earthly beauty.

§

Not for gold or jewels will Truth come your way;
Opening your heart is the price you must pay.

Lives without a purpose are empty and hollow;
Transcending the mind is the path you should follow.

Seek the peace of the sages and in others find
The One Supreme Truth, within all mankind.

§

The path of love is difficult to pledge,
Like walking carefully on a razor's edge.

Falling are those not yet ready;
To cross one must be calm and steady.

§

True dedication to the sages is difficult to acquire;
Like walking a path through a roaring fire.

To pass through safely, never hesitate,
For consumed are those who doubt and wait.

§

Such individuals, wanting worldly pleasures,
Do not gain spiritual treasures.

A true devotee, let it be known,
By remaining detached, loves the Truth alone.

§

Dawn has begun
With the rising sun.

Tenacious habits go away
As the Guide shows the way.

Wisdom vanishes and can't be found
Whenever greed does abound.

See how devotion does swiftly depart
When pride festers, consuming the heart.

§

When devotion to the guru is not utterly sincere,
Then your birth is worthless on the earth, says Kabir.

The shapes in the mist appear to be something,
But quickly they dissipate into nothing.

§

To the Lord of love alone direct your devotion,
Leaving aside all petty emotion.

The insincere student leaves as adversity does begin
Like a snake sheds his old, dead skin.

§

Practice

If the student doesn't his practice start,
What can the guru do; he has done his part.

The Word is imparted to the student,
But not retained, as it was meant.

Once the instrument is broken in some way,
Who could ever such an instrument play?

§

So sweet the words that come from you,
But opposing actions you often do.

Through silence you are able to see
Your actions as they ought to be.

All impurities are cleansed away
And virtuous deeds you then display.

§

It's not hard to withstand a blazing fire;
While dueling with sword, you may never tire.

But it's a most difficult task to do,
Keeping love for the Lord sincere and true.

§

Kabir destroyed the ego's fortress;
The passions five he did dismiss.

With the sharp, piercing sword of realization in hand,
Of the tangled knot of karma, he did loosen each strand.

§

Kabir, real warriors do not desert the battlefield;
Mind and illusion they fight with sword and shield.

To please his master he does aspire,
But to kill or be killed he does not desire.

§

If you have escaped far away,
Freedom shall never come your way.

Kabir says: One must stand for what is right;
Firmly the senses you must fight.

§

Once the brave soldier surrendered his feelings and mind,
Once his desire to live can no longer bind—

With open arms the teacher will then accept
His new disciple, ready to be adept.

§

Feed the ego,
The ego will grow.

Says Kabir: Cut the ego, purify your mind
And the luminous light you will find.

The lantern will become more bright
When the wick is trim and tight.

§

Let fear of God grow,
Then all other fears go.

When fear of God does fade,
Then other fears pervade.

Once fear of God has been lost,
By the mire of delusion man is tossed.

§

Pride brings forth a deep sea of problems.
Kabir says: From ego, all suffering stems.

Kindness makes possible a harmony restored;
Through forgiveness then, one realizes the Lord.

§

If learning to forgive you never attain,
Profound and peaceful you can never remain.

One can chatter and talk all day,
But with no forgiveness, contentment cannot stay.

§

Don't wait until tomorrow, do it today.
Whatever you are doing now, do it right away.

Later it will be too late to do;
Who knows when death will visit you?

§

Many desire to battle and fight;
Many boast of their conquests of war with delight.

But, alas, a mere few will stand and not bend,
Who want to attain peace, and strive to the end.

§

Kabir says: The true hero, you will find,
Is one in control of his own mind.

He, who control over the five senses does gain,
Removes the source of problems and pain.

§

Says Kabir: Mere talk is no help to you;
Infinitely more important is what you do.

Only through action, possible can it be,
That you can be ferried cross the dark, rough sea.

§

Who sits and talks and makes no effort,
Will never receive the spiritual comfort.

Mere talk of food never will,
All one's hunger satisfy and fill.

§

The real servant serves from his heart,
Not expecting anything for doing his part.

A good student one can never be
Without serving others selflessly.

§

Study is good, I will say,
But meditation is a better way.

Dedication to practice I hold strong,
Even if people insist I am wrong.

§

Once the fury of pride has died away
And the fuel of desire has burned its last day,

Once the drum of gloating has played its last beat
And the mind in silence is now complete;

When the strings, once played, have snapped in two—
Sound from the instrument will not come through.

Man's own problems he always makes
By repeating his foolish, petty mistakes.

Once all is seen clearly in the light that shines bright,
He shall forget all argument and cease to fight.

Kabir says: The highest goal is close to those
From whom peace and contentment constantly flow.

§

Faith

Fear and anxiety are a useless pair;
Says Kabir: They never lead me anywhere.

The Lord now takes good care of me;
From worries and anxiety I am free.

The Lord provides for all, everywhere—
The wild animals, insects, and birds in the air.

Fret not about this anxiety and fear;
The Lord gives to thee, too, says Kabir.

§

For the fortunate whose faith is deep,
Nothing they hoard, nothing they keep.

They have faith that the Lord will provide each day.
This Almighty Lord always gives in every way.

§

Desire for the Lord

The world sleeps deep with indifference,
Still pacified in its ignorance.

Kabir sleeps not, but he weeps,
Constant sight on the Lord he keeps.

§

The suffering body goes through stress and strain
But one pierced by love has a peculiar pain.

Kabir says: Love in this body dwells,
And my heart this pain swells.

§

What A Sage Does

It rains for all, on all the same,
Whether filled with pride or filled with shame.

The sage acts in a different way,
Cleansing all fears and passions away.

§

The guru is beyond maya's beck and call,
No one is enemy, he honors all.

He removes our pains and forgives our mistakes;
He asks for nothing, no gifts he takes.

§

To the great sage, pain and pleasure are equal;
Selflessly giving, he's a perfect example.

Serving all who seek his counsel and advice,
Always ready, his teaching is clear and concise.

Such a great one you should seek out;
Surrender of ego removes all doubt.

But seldom do such sages appear;
Fortunate is he who finds one, says Kabir.

§

The fruit ripens, but not for the tree;
The river gathers water for the ocean or the sea.

Only for the others' sake
Does a sage a human form take.

§

The Rare Sages

Kabir says: Many trees in the forest stood,
But not in every forest grows the sandalwood.

Pearls are precious, lustrous and round,
But not in all seas are they found.

The same with a sage, one most rare—
They are not found everywhere.

§

Alone, the lion prefers the serene;
With a herd he will never be seen.

In flocks, swans are not known to fly;
A true hero seldom passes by.

So among the masses common and strong,
The sages rarely ever come along.

§

The Lord Divine

Just as oil is squeezed from a mustard seed,
As from a flintstone a spark will proceed,

Within you the Lord dwells in Bliss;
Wake from your sleep and realize this.

§

If I say He is heavy, it would be untrue.
If I say He is light, I'd be wrong too.

About the Lord what can I say?
I've never seen Him in any form or way.

§

To say the Lord is one is not true;
It's also a lie to say He is two.

Kabir shares knowledge that is his:
That the Lord is only who He is.

§

If the Lord were to appear before me
What kind of description could there be?

If an effort is made to describe what I see
Do you think anyone would believe in me?

The Lord is who He is;
Revere Him, sing the praises which are His.

§

We become so attached and attracted to the shells
That we forget the pearl, which within us dwells.

Kabir says: The Lord's form does take place,
But not in the forms that we embrace.

§

The light is in the eye—not outside;
Within us all does the Lord reside.

But in our search for God,
All over the world we have trod.

§

The holy sage maintains his poise
Even among the evil and their noise.

See the vipers hang in the sandalwood tree—
Yet the sandal fragrance flows unceasingly.

§

An ant was carrying a tiny seed,
When he saw a rice grain that he also did need.

"How to hold both?" The ant did ask.
Kabir says: It's not possible to do such a task.

It must take one and the other lose,
As between God and the world, the disciple must choose.

§

When the Lord is your master and shows the way,
How can fears have any sway?

Those riding high on an elephant's back know,
The barking dogs can't bother them from below.

§

Within all milk, is the ghee;
Within all creation, so is He.

Many speak and many hear
About this analogy, says Kabir.

But one who churns the Self is rare indeed,
In his spiritual practice he does succeed.

§

A brightly colored picture is the world that we see;
Ignore the picture; let your awareness on the Painter be.

§

It's similar, when you a sage go near,
To visiting a perfume shop, says Kabir.

Although you may not buy a single thing,
The scent remains upon you, lingering.

§

Between a sage and a fake, a difference there be,
Just as between the mango and the thorny *babul* tree:

Luscious fruit, the mango adorns,
While the babul yields only spiny thorns.

§

Whatever you see does pass away;
Contemplate on the unseen along the way.

Once the key to the doorless gate is gifted,[1]
Then the veil that hides the Lord is lifted.

§

[1]The "doorless gate," in yogic philosophy, refers to the tenth gate at
the crown of the head, through which the soul is believed to enter and
exit the body.

§

The sage, like a river, is ever-flowing;
Love is the water, over-flowing.

Cleanse yourself in this water so pure,
By keeping company with sages, says Kabir.

§

Dwelling in the Lord

Kabir, your sincere devotion dwells deep,
But your mischievous mind, control does keep.

Your mind's senses you have always adored,
Yet you presume to be faithful to the Lord.

§

Now I have mastered my senses and mind;
Now I find myself inseparably aligned.

Now my whole being is purified;
I find the Splendid One residing inside.

§

If sensual pleasures play the most important part,
How can the Lord ever dwell in your heart?

When the Lord dwells within you,
All sensual pleasures disperse, too.

§

Kabir, your heart will not the Summit attain,
As long as delusion persists and remains.

Between the lover and his Lord
One should establish an unbroken cord.

The Lord will not let anything pass,
Not even a single blade of grass.

§

In the cave of heart the Lord chooses to reside—
Where can such a heart from the world hide?

Though one tries to hide from view,
Somehow the light always shines through.

§

A place where birth and death have no say,
Where the power of death no longer can sway,

Go, Kabir, to the place of tranquility and peace,
Where healed by the Lord, all problems will cease.

§

Scriptures, man can learn to memorize,
But this is quite a wasteful exercise.

Jewelry and fancy clothes, it would be a mistake,
To think they ever would an attractive beauty make.

An attractive woman is not made from silk and lace,
Her beauty is attained by spiritual grace.

§

Realization

Can a person ever explain
The taste of sugar, simple and plain?

Knowledge of realization is the same way;
Once the disciple tastes, what can he say?

§

Once perfect knowledge of your Self you can claim,
Pleasant and unpleasant all appear the same.

Once the enlightened heart, shining light sends,
All argument, lectures, and useless talk ends.

§

Once Self-realization is attained,
All writing and describing are restrained.

The one who writes still lives on this earth;
Realization frees one from the bondage of death and
    birth.

§

My master destroyed all that I thought mattered;
All pride and myths were completely shattered.

All my practices did go,
My beads, my books, and ego.

§

Drunk from the goblet of Supreme Bliss,
His enchantment in the Lord's love is endless.

Like an elephant he fearlessly roams around,
Without pain, but with joy that has no bound.

§

Lord's Name

A barn full of hay is so easily lost,
If a single glowing ember into the hay is tossed.

The Lord's name, once it has the heart entered in,
Instantly incinerates all old sin.

§

Hide your vision of the Lord:
Deep in your heart, keep it stored.

If you try to describe what you perceive,
Don't think you'll find anyone who'll believe.

§

To be one with the Lord is hard to do,
Yet continue at a rate that is right for you;

Soft but firm each step should be,
Then oneness with the Lord you shall certainly see.

§

Devotion I could not steadily continue;
Strength from within did not ensue.

All accomplishments are only His,
And hence Kabir is how he is.

§

Everything happens as Providence plans;
Nothing will stand if planned by man.

Man is the architect of his own fate
But he uses the intelligence of He who is great.

§

Whatever you do, my friend,
Do that which brings your pain to an end.

Cease this foolish, petty play;
Don't let sense pleasures have their way.

§

The world burns in the fire,
Of attachment and desire.

Why must you jump into this flame,
Like all the others, suffer the same?

§

You cry for God from the bottom of your heart;
You are essentially His inseparable part.

In the sages' company you should be;
Converse with them, the truth to see.

§

O my friends, do not me doubt,
From this treacherous pain there is a way out:
The Lord's name you must attain,
For it alone will destroy the pain.

The Lord's name alone is the support and aid,
In this world where pain does pervade;
The Lord's name is the rescue boat,
That crosses the ocean, still afloat.

§

Firmly hold the Lord's name,
Magnificent with eternal fame.

If you forsake the Lord, how will your life flow?
There is not actually anywhere else to go.

Move according to your own will and fashion,
You'll be burned like a moth by the fire of passion.

Sense pleasures are worse than a viper's venom;
Protect yourself from the poison of them.

§

Shoreless, bottomless, and upsurging fast,
This dark world-ocean is so vast!

Prepare yourself to be kept afloat,
Cross to joyful banks in the master's boat.

The currents and cross-currents of passions and desires,
Pull the mind under, into a confusing quagmire.

Stuck amongst these roaring waves and foam,
There is no way to get back home.

The sea of existence has no bottom,
So mysteriously dark one can't fathom.

The only help and support man can claim,
Is placing full faith in the Lord's name.

Kabir says: Once the Lord gave me His protection,
Then I viewed the world from a different direction.

This bottomless dark ocean was made insignificant
    somehow;
So small, it became a hoofprint puddle left behind by a cow.

§

Flames can't scorch it;
Thieves don't approach it.

By the wind it can't be tossed;
For the Lord's name cannot be lost.

§

Oneness

When soul is wedded to the Lord they are inseparably
  One;
Inexplicable it is, the disciple's task is done.

There is no difference between Thee and me;
For now, everything is melted in Thee.

Kabir says: Like two metals joined as one,
Between Him and me there is no distinction.

§

The "me" can no longer play a chord,
For now only Thou exist, my Lord.

I no longer am, only Thou art;
I no longer am, only Thou art.

§

Says Kabir: To the master of all,
He who is highest, hear my call—

I am dead to the world's lethal sins.
Yet dead I am not to the spiritual life within.

Once again the Lord is all in One,
For I exist not; my pilgrimage is done.

§

From the same blood are we;
Only one life flows through Thee and me.

For the birth of the world one mother we credit;
Where does the idea come, which makes us separate?

We all are the spark of the blazing light;
Let all enjoy spiritual delight!

Split by the evil pressures of the world,
Into many divisions and sects, we have unfurled.

§

The fire of love was kindled anew,
And into the space a brilliant spark flew.

Once the spark and the Absolute, together had come,
Then finally, one with It, had the spark become.

§

Says Kabir: Many brave warriors I have met,
But those pierced with love, none as yet.

When two wounded with love for the Lover relate,
It's not possible to describe the music they create.

§

Through Love—
And Not Renunciation

If being naked were the qualification
That would surely bring us liberation;

Then wild animals fulfill the prerequisite
And they would be the first to attain it.

§

If celibacy could lead to liberation
Then the eunuchs need no preparation.

Those who gain liberation, please hear,
Have obtained the Lord's name, says Kabir.

§

How simple would be the path to tread
If one could be enlightened by having shaven head.

See the distance a sheep is from the Lord sublime,
Though the sheep is shaved from time to time.

§

Telling mala beads the whole day through,
Thinking shaving your head is the thing to do,

Wearing orange clothes is only fleeing—
For none of these things makes a holy being.

§

Telling Beads

Since ancient times many men
Have told their beads again and again,

But their wandering minds led them astray,
For their minds found no rest that way.

Says Kabir: Put those beads from your fingers aside;
Let the internal japa be your mind's guide.

§

Truly your fingers are occupied,
Busy, telling each bead aside.

But can't you hear your heart pound
As passion's fire leaps all around?

Just as a man trying to run on the street
Only falls flat with frostbitten feet.

§

Mind

Kabir, don't be misled by the mind;
Leave this ancient habit behind.

Endless are its tricky plays;
Clever and crafty are its ways.

One whose mind is under control
Certainly is a rare soul.

§

By doing nothing you will not the Lord's grace gain;
By babbling silly words you will not Him attain.

You must free yourself from your mind's sway
If you want the Lord's name to show you the way.

§

Kabir speaks lucid and plain;
He warns everybody, but in vain:

Men are hoping to cross the sea without fail
By blindly grasping at a sheep's tail.

§

Don't allow wealth to make you delighted;
Don't allow conflict to make you excited.

Toward joy and sorrow take the same stand:
Everything happens by the Lord's command.

§

For pleasure and comfort have no desire;
Have no fear of pain and hell's fire.

All that is to be,
Will happen purposefully.

Put not your mind in such a strain—
Dreaming empty dreams with nothing to gain.

§

The mind already knows all,
Yet to bad habits does it fall.

What's the purpose of a lantern, anyway,
If you do not use it to light the way?

§

You were not there when my ego was strong;
My ego was gone once You came along.

So narrow and slender is love's lane,
That two together, it could never contain.

§

Lustful Life

The lustful person lives in illusion;
He never finds freedom from doubt and delusion.

Lust separates the victim from the Lord;
This division results from lust's cruel sword.

§

If lust, anger, greed, and ego, on their own,
Rule the mind and control the throne,

Whether one is a king or of scholarly fame—
In reality, they are one and the same.

§

Wherever lust comes to reside
The Lord's name won't preside.

Wherever the Lord's name is in control
Lust cannot play its ugly role.

Light and darkness, space never share;
When one is present, the other is not there.

§

Greed and Desires

Greed is a whore who never wears out;
She is not one to be near about.

If it's your heart you've let her in,
She'll slow your every move and lead you to sin.

§

The blazing fire of greed
Will never quite recede;

If the water of satisfaction flows
Daily this fire only grows.

But douse the flame with love and devotion;
Wash off this gripping, misleading emotion—

Then death will come to greed and its pain,
Like the *jawasa* shedding its leaves in the rain.[2]

[2]The jawasa plant is known to shed its leaves during heavy
rainshowers.

§

Greed is a treacherous demon,
Causing downfall to many men.

"More and more" is its eternal drone;
The seeds of sorrow it has sown.

§

When desires dry and go away,
Worries have no space to stay;

Then the mind is tranquil and free of all things.
He who has no desires is higher than kings.

§

Diamonds, rubies, mansions, and gold,
And all the wealth the world can hold—

All these finally go to dust;
For peace, contentment is a must.

§

Anger

Anger sets the world afire;
The flames burn the world entire.

Protection is complete with the practice of His name,
From the fire that is sparked by anger's flame.

§

Anger is a barrier on the spiritual path;
Much harm is created by anger or wrath.

Spiritual accomplishments are dissipated
When ego spurs anger to be created.

§

Sincere forgiveness stops and releases
Anger into powerless pieces.

One who will give, show compassion, and understand
Remains untrapped by time's command.

§

Malicious words hurt and burn with their thrust,
Leaving the other burnt to ashes and dust.

Only soothing, peaceful words the master will give
To those who are reborn and want to live.

§

Attachment

Only darkness exists
Where attachment persists.

By the truly faithful alone
Will the Truth be known.

It enters through detachment's door,
Then crosses to the luminous shore.

§

So fierce is attachment's pull and sway,
It has great men and intellectuals swept away.

But the pure and truly loving one
Will in the end the goal have won

If, as a small fish swimming from the deep,
Conscience and purpose in front does keep.

§

Wearing silks of the latest style,
Dining on the richest meals worthwhile—

Yet, says Kabir, without God's name,
You'll be burnt by hell's flame.

§

Just Criticism

O Kabir, there are those sad, slandering souls
For whom love of God is not the goal.

Then there are those immersed in the Lord's name
Who long to be near His blazing flame.

§

Fools ridicule and joke of others' imperfections
But never try to correct their own reflections.

§

Fear not, the slanderer will live forever;
May death not come for him, ever.

The slanderer's words revealed the sight,
Assisting Kabir to realize His Light.

§

Slandering a sage is a terrible sin;
There the path of sorrow does begin.

In the eternal fury of sin he dwells;
Lacking liberation, his ego swells.

§

Boasting of yourself you should not do;
Slandering others should not be your view.

This journey is long before its end;
It's unknown what waits around the bend.

§

Don't brood on others' faults, says Kabir;
See their merits and these, alone, do cheer.

Collect the nectar, like a bee;
In everyone's heart, the Lord you should see.

§

Useless Chatter

Once I reach the other side
The journey I will to you confide.

But the boat now rocks upon the sea;
Talk of it echoes uselessly.

§

Much misery comes from arguments,
Slander, rudeness, and disagreements.

In silence the sage finds only peace;
All anger, strife, and conflicts cease.

§

Allowing spiritual ideas to be unfurled
To people bound to the mundane world,

Is like a barren woman rocking to and fro,
An empty cradle, with nothing to show—

Kabir asks: How can this be gratifying?
Nothing like that will be satisfying!

§

About God there is much speech and chatter
But something bothers me in this matter:

How can they God's acquaintance make
When they do nothing for His sake?

§

Pride of Body or Self

Thy mortal body, take no pride in—
It's just many bones in a bag of skin.

Riders of royal elephants with a golden crest—
Even they will be buried for final rest.

§

Why be vain, asks Kabir,
Of your beautiful mansion you hold so dear?

For any time now, death will put you in the ground;
Then green grass growing over your head will abound.

§

Like a bubble in the froth on the sea
Your existence short and fleeting will be.

Soon you'll no longer be, and in a flash you'll go,
Just as the stars disappear as the morning light does glow.

§

What good does your large size do
If its purpose is of little value?

The palm tree stands strong and tall;
Its fruit no one can reach at all.

Nothing to provide shade for rest—
It's a useless, standing stump, at best.

§

Love you are always seeking;
Yet pride you are always keeping.

Impossible, that love and pride,
Together truly can reside.

How can two swords, one sheath share?
Ridiculous to make such a pair.

§

One who has tasted the love Divine,
His heart becomes a living shrine;

With gem on palm, you shouldn't go
Out on the street for public show.

§

The mindful woman with jar on her head—
Is higher than the queen, holding pride instead.

The queen has magnificent elephants to ride,
And well-bred horses are ridden with pride.

§

In this world we sojourn for a brief stay,
But to our wealth and knowledge we constantly fall prey.

Death brings us all to the same end,
Whether a king or a pauper, foe or friend.

§

Kabir says, the abode of the Lord of Love, I do treasure
As a shrine of the divine, not a house of pleasure.

O friend! surrender all your pride
If you ever yearn to know the Lord inside.

§

Maya

So many scholars well-versed in the scriptures—
They cannot unfold themselves, these miserable creatures.

For what these experts have come to know,
Only out of ignorance does it grow.

The elephant described by men who are blind,
A partial interpretation does each find.

Intuitive knowledge flows through the master
Saving one from spiritual disaster.

§

An ignorant king was reborn as a mule
Slavishly carrying wood for fuel.

Though exhausted by work, he was never fed
Since exploiting others was the life he had led.

§

Under the mire of delusion, you know not what to
    believe;
Calm down so you can see, yourself you have deceived:

In a house of mirrors a dog is set free;
He barks at his own reflection, which he does see—

Then there's a lion looking in a well
Who jumps at his own reflection because he can't tell—

Or the greedy monkey who holds so tight
But is trapped by holding with all his greedy might—

Like a parrot firmly holding the branch,
Not anyone's slave but in its own trance—

Maya makes us slave and creates a chasm of fear;
Taking shadow as real, your attachments you hold dear.

§

Remember, warns Kabir:
No one is your true friend;
Everyone has his selfish end.

The undisciplined mind is filled with confusion;
It doesn't see this world as only an illusion.

§

In the spell of a dream from which it can't wake,
The world can't differentiate a sage from a fake.

When you see a crowd following someone,
He is not necessarily a holy one.

§

Many worries and problems come about
Because of possessions and silly doubt.

Anger builds and you blow steam;
Suddenly you waken from your dream.

All the possessions and things you hoard
Shall only separate you from the Lord.

§

As a moth flutters into the light,
It dies in the flame at night.
Precious life is lost in confusion,
Vainly chasing mirages and illusion.

A true guru alone guides the way,
Destroying the fetters of dismay.

§

In searching for the Lord, the bird of life flies,
While the Inner Dweller, within the heart lies.

Maya blindfolds and robs your sight;
You can not see either Him or His light.

§

Kabir is so intoxicated with the Lord's name,
He is transformed; he is not the same.

Once the potter's bowl has met the fire's burn,
Never again on the wheel must it turn.

§

A prince in a royal family—
Yet a thief, you turn out to be.

When poison fills a chalice that's jewel-bedecked,
Does it still hold the same awe and respect?

§

Many kings together cannot rule a peaceful land;
Only one ruler in the mind may stand.

Happiness is not found in a kingdom divided,
Nor in a person whom maya misguided.

§

What good does burning incense to idols do,
Or soaking your clothes in holy water, too?

Aware that I must drop this body someday,
Let me not forget this is a game and a play.

§

I only see, as I look all around,
Those who to worldly ways are bound
Even great orators, meditators, and the wise
Are blinded by the world's disguise.

Kabir says: When the name of the Lord does not prevail
Reality is hidden by maya's veil.

§

Stone Idols

Sculptured stone standing on a block—
As if the Lord, men worship this rock.

Those trusting such rocks will quickly be
Drowned in tides of the dark, mournful sea.

§

Where does worshipping stone idols lead?
How can a rock answer a prayer, indeed?

It is the foolish who crave for material gain;
Their desire for spiritual growth, lost in vain.

§

Unknowingly, I would have begged rock idols for their
  graces,
And then wandered about, visiting temples and holy
  places.

But by Master's love and grace did I awaken;
Through him this load from my head has been taken.

§

Men are always trying to amass riches,
Revering idols as religious crutches.

The salesmen use their tactics and say
That these rocks are the Lord in every way.

So with your money one of these idols you buy,
But it turns out lifeless, cold—a rock that's dry.

Carving a rock does not the Lord make;
Such foolish practices, please forsake.

§

Worshipping water and rock are ridiculous;
All such worship proves itself fruitless.

Revere men of God and faithfully serve;
Remember His name, with each breath you observe.

§

It's not possible to purify within
By bathing at holy places; no one washes sin.

By impressing others, you will nothing achieve;
You are not fooling the Lord; He is not naive.

§

The One Absolute you should adore;
Realize this and one thing more:

Serving the teacher is the only way;
With all humility you must pray.

§

If bathing in holy water can to liberation lead,
What of all the frogs that in the water swim and breed?

The men come to bathe just as the frogs do;
And like the frogs, they'll be born again, too.

§

Where neither day nor night are cast—
Where neither holy books nor scriptures last—

Where the ocean neither falls nor swells—
Eternally calm, there the Splendid One dwells.

Place your faith in that Absolute One,
Who dwells in the heart of everyone.

Place your faith in that One, says Kabir;
Toward this insane world, don't go near.

§

Many religious pilgrimages one might make,
And thousands of visits for ritual's sake.

But until one learns from a spiritual master,
One cannot be saved from spiritual disaster.

§

If by worshipping rock the Lord can be found,
To the worship of a mount I am bound.

Better than these idols that are from stone born,
Are the useful stones that grind the corn.

§

Religion

If men are Muslim only by circumcision,
How are women considered in this decision?

Since your better half is with you,
You still remain a Hindu.

§

After the sacred thread ceremony a man becomes
    Brahmin.
But when is the ceremony ever given for a woman?

She is a Shudra by birth, you must admit;
How can you eat the food she serves, O Pandit?

§

Conforming to rules that religion does lay,
Is like a baby who with its toys does play.

It's hard to quit playing the role of life's drama,
Unless your heart is free from *kama*.[3]

§

After collecting rock, cement, and sand,
A mosque is built from what's been planned.

At the top of the mosque the mullah shouts,
So his prayer can be heard without any doubts.

But, I ask of you, mullah, what do you fear,
Do you think the great Lord above can't hear?

§

O mullah, you climb to the top of the stairs
And into the air you shout your prayers.

Don't ever think that the Lord can't hear;
He is not deaf but has infinite ears.

§

To this Lord you spend many hours praying.
Your prayers are unheard, what are you saying?

Go within, to the depths of the heart;
There you become His inseparable part.

[3]In yoga philosophy kama refers to the basic desire, from which all
desires originate.

§

Says Kabir, if your spiritual guide is blind,
Impossible it is, to seek light and find.

When the blind, the way to the blind show,
Into the darkness both will go.

§

The night sky remains unlit by the sun;
All the stars shine and twinkle, every one.

It's the same as the men who don't God know,
Who are involved in vain rituals, and fruitless seeds sow.

§

How can you find where the path to the city lies,
When the guide himself in the grasp of ignorance cries?

When the boat is in a fierce uproar,
How will the passengers cross to the other shore?

§

If one does not know the Lord and his calling,
Then from heaven to hell, one is rising and falling.

Good and evil are the creations of mind;
Neither heaven nor hell do I care to find.

§

Those who boast to have known the Lord
Blindly grope for a two-edged sword.

Says Kabir: Yet, after all their seeking,
They know not of what they're speaking;

All speak of heaven and wish to go
But by such talk, they'll never know.

§

The Lord enters the seeker's heart
When pride has shattered and fallen apart.

If you for joys of heaven wait
Being with the Lord is not your fate.

§

The loyal wife loves only one Lord in life.
Love of many, makes a harlot, not a wife.

With whose body will you join at the funeral pyre,
Since many husbands you did acquire?

§

Great may the orator be, cultured and refined;
Self-centered and indignant, his learning stays confined.

Higher than the vulture does the Pandit's ego fly;
Both eventually descend, this they can't deny.

§

Many talk about the Lord
But much of this should be ignored.

Where will this boasting talk ever lead,
If they speak of the Lord who they do not heed?

§

To the Hindu faith I do not comply,
Nor a member of Islam am I.

Only of the five elements I am made;
Within this cave my soul has stayed.

§

Performing ceremonies is not the way,
For they are the same as any child's play.

Until you delight in the Lord's domain,
The Lord's face, veiled, from you will remain.

§

Pompous Scholars

Despite all his scriptures a scholar has no advantage;
All such learning is like a trained parrot's knowledge.

A fortune teller's parrot, others' future unveils,
But in her own case, she miserably fails.

§

Kabir mocks the scholarly ones:
All these texts you keep reading
Are not what your heart is needing.

Self-deluded, you try to help others through your learning
And never attain that for which you are yearning.

§

They interpret the four Vedas throughout the day
But the Lord's love doesn't come their way.

Kabir has searched and kept only the grain;
Uselessly the scholars sift the remains.

§

Fatigue from reading too many pages
Never makes men realized sages.

But once the meaning of love is known,
The highest wisdom then is shown.

§

The parrot easily learns by rote,
The words of the scriptures how to quote.

A prisoner in its own wire cage,
Repeating wisdom from a written page—

While others applaud and say it's great,
The parrot never sees its imprisoned state.

§

Reading and reading, more and more,
Men become lifeless like rocks on the shore;

Writing and writing, on and on,
Like a brick, the intelligence is gone.

Kabir, these men playing scholarly parts,
Are lifeless, as love has not entered their hearts.

§

Through reading and pondering for a long time,
After studying and listening a whole lifetime,

Delusion remains; it will insist.
All such learning it can resist.

Such learning brings no real gain, says Kabir;
Rarely will someone this message hold dear.

§

Mere scriptural knowledge and shallow intellect,
Everywhere we find, easy to collect.

To conquer instead desire and lust,
To master the mind because you must,

To open the heart and make it pure—
These goals are higher, more difficult to secure.

§

O learned priest, your sermons are untrue;
By repeating *Ram* delusion you won't subdue.[4]

By muttering "sugar" again and again,
Can the tongue taste any sweetness, then?

---

[4]*Ram,*used here, refers to the name of one of the Hindu gods.

Words do not light the fire and make heat;
Such foolish thoughts won't warm your feet.

Simply by speaking of water, you insist
That your thirst will be quenched and cease to exist?

"Food" is all you need to say
Then your hunger goes away?

You see, of course, if this were only true,
Then by saying *Ram* maya's delusion would be through.

§

Saying *Hari, Hari* a trained parrot's knowledge shows,[5]
But of Hari's true nature the parrot does not know.

If the parrot from its cage were free
It would surely forget the name Hari.

§

What is accomplished by merely reciting God's name
Without the experience of knowing the same?

If saying "wealth" could money restore,
Then who would be rich and who would be poor?

§

[5]*Hari* refers to a name used by Hindus for an aspect of God.

O learned experts, your real desires and pleasures
Are for selfish wealth and earthly treasures.

You say, "Listen to me so your faith can be restored,"
But you laugh and mock true devotees of the Lord.

Says Kabir: If love for the one Lord you've forsaken,
Then to the lord of death you'll be taken.

§

To the learned how can one explain,
After self-realization, the wisdom you attain?

Such understanding doesn't come through the mind;
This is as useless as dancing for the blind.

§

The intellectual does not go within to learn;
Outside he searches but true knowledge spurns.

If he could realize the luminous Lord within,
His heavy tomes of learning would seem shallow and
   thin.

§

Scriptural regurgitation is useless, I find;
It still leaves you inexperienced and shamefully blind.
I report only what I experience and know
Realization is the path that the guru will show.

§

Surrender

With palms together, I pray to Thee,
Oh Lord, grant these kind blessings to me:

To be with the sages, their darshan to enjoy,
And to have a pure heart filled with love and joy.

§

O Lord, have pity on me—
I am caught in a raging sea.

Its crashing waves will wash me away—
Please Lord, save me from its sway.

§

How to sin I know too well;
My selfish thoughts are hard to quell.

Only the Lord can help me regain
Freedom from wickedness, suffering, and pain.

Lord, assist this sinner some way;
Save me from evil's powerful play.

§

Nothing is mine;
All this is Thine.

I surrender all to Thee;
Nothing more is left of me.

§

So many selfish acts I have done,
So little progress have I won.

I surrender Lord to Thee;
I'll do all you ask of me.

Punish or forgive me, I submit;
With me, do as You see fit.

§

The love of the Lord doesn't grow in the ground;
For sale in the market, it never is found.

All are entitled, the poor and the kings.
Surrender to God gives the lover's heart wings.

§

Within the body the Lord does reside
But you constantly look for Him outside.

In churches, in temples, in holy sites you look;
So you think you'll find him in a book?

Those who seek to know the Lord
Will find serenity restored.

§

Gurus and Masters

So many false gurus abound;
Few disciples are to be found.

There is a ray of hope, says Kabir,
When a disciple does finally appear.

§

Social status does not make any difference;
The wisdom alone should be your point of inference.

Why be misled by the beauty of the sheath,
When the sharpness of the sword lies beneath?

§

The guru and God are inseparably one;
Everything else is just an illusion.

Have freedom from ego's hold;
Be embraced within the guru's fold.

If it's the Lord you want to know,
Love and reverence you must show.

§

Blind and ignorant are those who do not think
That God and guru have an eternal link.

Deprived of the wisdom, they'll soon regret,
Caught in illusion's binding net.

§

The Lord appears in the form of master;
The goal of life is accomplished faster.

Bow down with reverence to his lotus feet;
Serve him with action and mind, complete.

By remembering God with every breath of life,
Enjoy his grace, attain freedom from strife.

§

If the master's task is to wash the fabric,
And the disciple is enveloped in dirt so thick,

Then the Word becomes the cleansing lotion,
Washing the mind with repetitive motion.

When the Word has purified the soul and mind
Such a rare student is hard to find.

§

When the master turns the potter's wheel,
He kneads the disciple—the clay—by feel:

Shaping the pot with intricate beauty,
Giving it a new shape is his duty.

With his gentle hands he hollows from within,
Holding the outside firmly as the wheel does spin.

§

Were I to see together the Lord and guru somehow,
To whom would it first be proper to bow?

No doubt my master's feet, for he
Revealed the Almighty Lord to me.

§

What has the disciple left to fear
In all three worlds, asks Kabir,

When he sees his master higher than all
And always obeys His orders and call.

§

It's a great accomplishment, you'll find,
When you offer actions, speech, and mind.

Set down the burden that you carry,
The heavy weight you always ferry.

§

The road to misery and pain you'll tread,
If by ignorance, you're blindly led.

The light of Providence to you will be shown
If you always remember the Lord alone.

§

When mind and action to the Lord you render,
Nothing more is left for you to surrender.

With all my being, here I declare,
I have nothing left to offer or share.

§

Be sure a seer is your spiritual guide,
A sage who is wise and dignified.

Be sure desires are brought under control,
That his ego does not play a conflicting role.

Death of his ego means he is reborn;
Free from conflict, your heart will never be torn.

There's more to surrender than one can see,
Subtler forces still must be.

§

The master alone can remove the veil
For the one who has learned how to curtail

The influences that separate and blind—
The unconscious, the body, and the mind.

Without the blinding veil, one has no fear.
It seldom happens, says Kabir.

§

Kabir reveals yet another little known fact:
Once the unconscious is surrendered and no longer can
   act,

All external temptations disappear from sight;
Everything vanishes except the guiding Light.

§

How can the master's greatness be described?
Even if the earth could be inscribed—

All the trees being the writing pens,
And oceans, the ink, to flow through them—

How can you describe his beauty sublime?
It is impossible for anyone to describe with rhyme.

§

Certainly all those fools remain ignorant and blind,
Who do not see the master as divine and kind.

One must not only remember the Lord but love the
    master too,
Then alone one experiences what is True.

For in an instant you will be lifted from maya's strong
    hold,
And then pulled past the three worlds' fold.

§

The master is the most selfless giver to be found;
The disciple is the poorest beggar around.

The master, to his sincere pupil very purely,
Bestows all the blessings very dearly.

Only the master can this gift bestow,
And through it the disciple will surely grow.

§

A truly holy person is one who
Is sensitive to the sufferings of others, too.

Then there are the self-centered, who insist
That others' needs don't even exist.

§

If man has no feet, how can he leap?
How can one rest if he doesn't sleep?

Without a mouth, how can I laugh?
Or make butter without a churning staff?

A cow without an udder, can no milk yield.
How can one journey if the road is concealed?

So, too, the spiritual path needs a guide:
Hear the teacher's message, deep inside.

§

Guidance

Many precious gems lie buried in rocky ground,
Seekers continue delving, hunting all around.

Seekers under the guru's direction and care
Collect many, while others standing there

Continue seeking through the grains of sand,
Yearning for gems, but returning with empty hand.

§

For those to whom is not yet known,
The difference between the guru and the *paras* stone:[6]

The stone will atoms into gold rearrange,
While the guru will the student completely change.

§

[6]In alchemy, a *paras* stone was thought to be able to turn other base
substances into gold.

In maya's maze all go 'round and 'round,
Looking for a way out that cannot be found.

Kabir says, only with the Lord's grace can it be done;
His grace will free you from this web you've spun.

§

Darshan

Religion, caste, and culture do not make a sage;
Spiritual attainment should be your only gauge.
See the sword; let the sheath be.
Ignore how he appears; only his wisdom see.

§

The time spent in a sage's company
Will benefit you throughout eternity.

If you ignore his guidance, you're wasting time;
The spiritual preceptor is one with God sublime.

§

Truly, the master's guidance you must gain;
From him, spiritual wealth you will attain.

Kabir warns: Never overlook the importance of this:
Converse with the sages, seek their love and bliss.

§

About Swami Rama

Yogi, scientist, philosopher, humanitarian, and mystic poet, Swami Rama is the founder and spiritual head of the Himalayan International Institute of Yoga Science and Philosophy, with its headquarters in Honesdale, Pennsylvania, and therapy and educational centers throughout the world. He was born in a Himalayan valley of Uttar Pradesh, India, in 1925 and was initiated and anointed in early childhood by a great sage of the Himalayas. He studied with many adepts, and then traveled to Tibet to study with his grandmaster. From 1949 to 1952 he held the prestige and dignity of Shankaracharya (spiritual leader) in Karvirpitham in the South of India. He then returned to the Himalayas to intensify his meditative practices in the cave monasteries and to establish an ashram in Rishikesh.

Later he continued his investigation of Western psychology and philosophy at several European universities, and he taught in Japan before coming to the United States in 1969. The

120

following year he served as a consultant to the Voluntary Controls Project of the Research Department of the Menninger Foundation. There he demonstrated, under laboratory conditions, precise control over his autonomic nervous system and brain. The findings of that research increased the scientific community's understanding of the human ability to control autonomic functioning and to attain previously unrecognized levels of consciousness.

Shortly thereafter, Swami Rama founded the Himalayan Institute as a means to synthesize the ancient teachings of the East with the modern approaches of the West. He has played a major role in bringing the insights of yoga psychology and philosophy to the attention of the physicians and psychologists of the West. He continues to teach students around the world while intensifying his writing and meditative practices. He is the author of many books and currently spends most of his time in the mountains of Northern India and in Pennsylvania, U.S.A.

Robert Regli was born in 1958 and grew up in Cupertino, California. After earning a Master's degree in Geology, Robert worked three years as an oil explorationist for a major oil company. He has studied yoga at the Himalayan Institute in Honesdale, Pennsylvania and has intensively studied yoga and Indian music in India. He has worked with Swami Rama on several texts from the Sikh tradition. Robert has also been writing poetry for over fifteen years.

The main building of the national headquarters, Honesdale, Pa.

The Himalayan Institute

The Himalayan International Institute of Yoga Science and Philosophy of the U.S.A. is a nonprofit organization devoted to the scientific and spiritual progress of modern humanity. Founded in 1971 by Sri Swami Rama, the Institute combines Western and Eastern teachings and techniques to develop educational, therapeutic, and research programs for serving people in today's world. The goals of the Institute are to teach meditational techniques for the growth of individuals and their society, to make known the harmonious view of world religions and philosophies, and to undertake scientific research for the benefit of humankind.

This challenging task is met by people of all ages, all walks of life, and all faiths who attend and participate in the Institute courses and seminars. These programs, which are given on a continuing basis, are designed in order that one may discover for oneself how to live more creatively. In the words of Swami Rama, "By being aware of one's own potential and abilities, one can become a perfect citizen, help the nation, and serve humanity."

The Institute has branch centers and affiliates throughout the United States. The 422-acre campus of the national headquarters, located in the Pocono Mountains of northeastern Pennsylvania, serves as the coordination center for all the Institute activities, which include a wide variety of innovative programs in education, research, and therapy, combining Eastern and Western approaches to self-awareness and self-directed change.

SEMINARS, LECTURES, WORKSHOPS, and CLASSES are available throughout the year, providing intensive training and experience in such topics as Superconscious Meditation, hatha yoga, philosophy, psychology, and various aspects of personal growth and holistic health. The *Himalayan Institute Quarterly Guide to Classes and Other Offerings* is sent free of charge to everyone on the Institute's mailing list.

The RESIDENTIAL and SELF-TRANSFORMATION PROGRAMS provide training in the basic yoga disciplines—diet, ethical behavior, hatha yoga, and meditation. Students are also given guidance in a philosophy of living in a community environment.

The PROGRAM IN HOLISTIC STUDIES offers a unique and systematic synthesis of Western empirical sources and Eastern introspective science. Graduate-level studies may be pursued through cross-registration with several accredited colleges and universities.

The five-day STRESS MANAGEMENT/PHYSICAL FITNESS PROGRAM offers practical and individualized training that can be used to control the stress response. This includes biofeedback, relaxation skills, exercise, diet, breathing techniques, and meditation.

A yearly INTERNATIONAL CONGRESS, sponsored by the Institute, is devoted to the scientific and spiritual progress of modern humanity. Through lectures, workshops, seminars, and practical demonstrations, it provides a forum for professionals and lay people to share their knowledge and research.

The ELEANOR N. DANA RESEARCH LABORATORY is the psychophysiological laboratory of the Institute, specializing in research on breathing, meditation, holistic therapies, and stress and relaxed states. The laboratory is fully equipped for exercise stress testing and psychophysiological measurements, including brain waves, patterns of respiration, heart rate changes, and muscle tension. The staff investigates Eastern teachings through studies based on Western experimental techniques.

Himalayan Institute Publications

Mantra and Meditation	Usharbudh Arya, D.Litt.
Philosophy of Hatha Yoga	Usharbudh Arya, D.Litt.
Meditation and the Art of Dying	Usharbudh Arya, D.Litt.
God	Usharbudh Arya, D.Litt.
Psychotherapy East and West: A Unifying Paradigm	Swami Ajaya, Ph.D.
Yoga Psychology	Swami Ajaya, Ph.D.
Psychology East and West	Swami Ajaya, Ph.D. (ed.)
Diet and Nutrition	Rudolph Ballentine, M.D.
Joints and Glands Exercises	Rudolph Ballentine, M.D. (ed.)
Transition to Vegetarianism	Rudolph Ballentine, M.D.
Theory and Practice of Meditation	Rudolph Ballentine, M.D. (ed.)
Freedom from Stress	Phil Nuernberger, Ph.D.
Science Studies Yoga	James Funderburk, Ph.D.
Homeopathic Remedies	Drs. Anderson, Buegel, Chernin
Hatha Yoga Manual I	Samskrti and Veda
Hatha Yoga Manual II	Samskrti and Judith Franks
Seven Systems of Indian Philosophy	Rajmani Tigunait, Ph.D.
Swami Rama of the Himalayas	L. K. Misra, Ph.D. (ed.)
Sikh Gurus	K.S. Duggal
Philosophy and Faith of Sikhism	K.S. Duggal
The Quiet Mind	John Harvey, Ph.D. (ed.)
Himalayan Mountain Cookery	Martha Ballentine
The Yoga Way Cookbook	Himalayan Institute
Meditation in Christianity	Himalayan Institute
Art and Science of Meditation	Himalayan Institute
Inner Paths	Himalayan Institute
Chants from Eternity	Himalayan Institute

To order or to request a free mail order catalog call or write
The Himalayan Publishers
RR 1, Box 400
Honesdale, PA 18431
Toll-Free 1-800-444-5772